# My Two Cats

## Jill Beth Miller

Close-up of Bernie
sniffing Max's tail.

Here are Max and
Bernie. Bernie is sniffing
Max's tail.

**FCP**

*Full Court Press*
*Englewood Cliffs, New Jersey*

To My Feline Babies, My Human Babies, And My Husband,
*with love and gratitude.*


*First Edition*

Published in the United States of America
by Full Court Press, 601 Palisade Avenue,
Englewood Cliffs, NJ 07632
fullcourtpress.com


ISBN 978-1-953728-17-3

*Editing and book design by Barry Sheinkopf*

She was much thinner from not having had enough to eat.

I found Max in a stairwell outside my apartment building.

She had also had her front paws de-clawed. This is mean to a cat. Without claws, a cat can't protect itself.

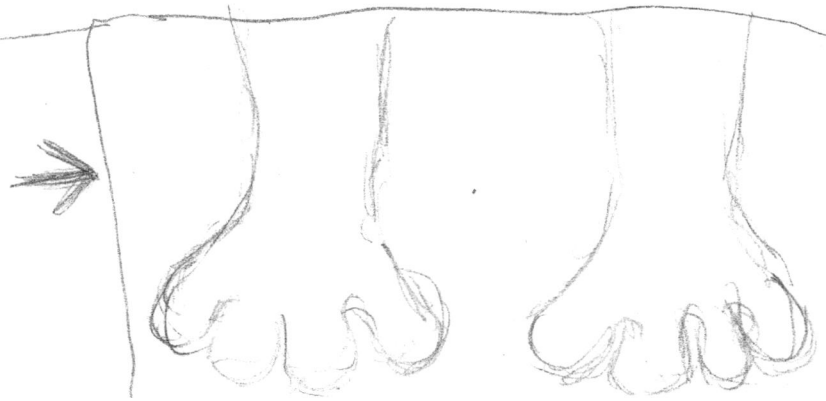

Cats also use their claws to climb.

Max had also been spayed. This is a good procedure that helps cats (and dogs) avoid getting pregnant. It's a good alternative to kitty condoms, which have not been invented and probably never will be.

Hubba...
Hubba!

Max is a female. Her name is not Maxine, Maxerella, Maxetta, or Minnie-Max. Why name a girl cat Max? I like the name!

I live in New York City

If I had a back yard or front lawn, Max could go outside.

MAX

Since I'm in the big city, Max is an indoor or "house cat." This is sort of funny, since I don't have a house.

Maybe we should call her an "apartment cat."

max

← me

During the day, I go to work.

It made me sad to leave Max alone all day.

What I imagined Max might do in my absence:

Meow. Meow - Meow *

* Translation : "I've so lonely. Come home soon."

What she probably did:

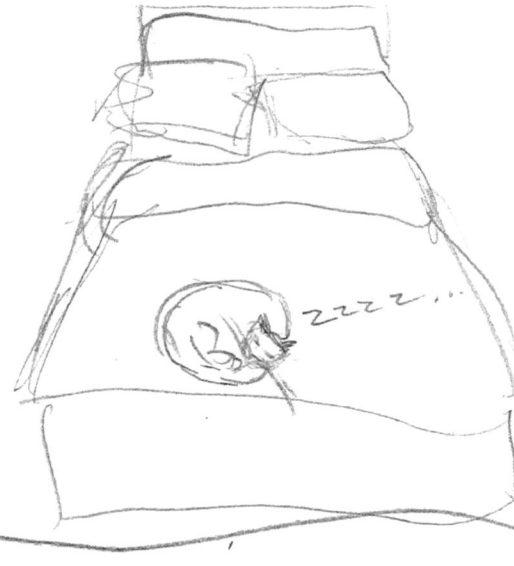

zzzz....

6

So I adopted Bernie! Now Max had a new friend!

Bernie was a kitten when he joined our family.

Bernie was only four months old.

Meow. Meow *

*Translation: "Ga Ga. Goo Goo."

Bernie is a male cat. He came with claws, which he's keeping (though I do trim them sometimes). I had him neutered so, like Max, he can't make babies. You could go to a library or a bookstore to learn more about how you can help prevent overpopulation of cats and dogs.

Too Many Cats
Too Little Food
by Dr. Katz

It took Max a
little while to get
used to Bernie.

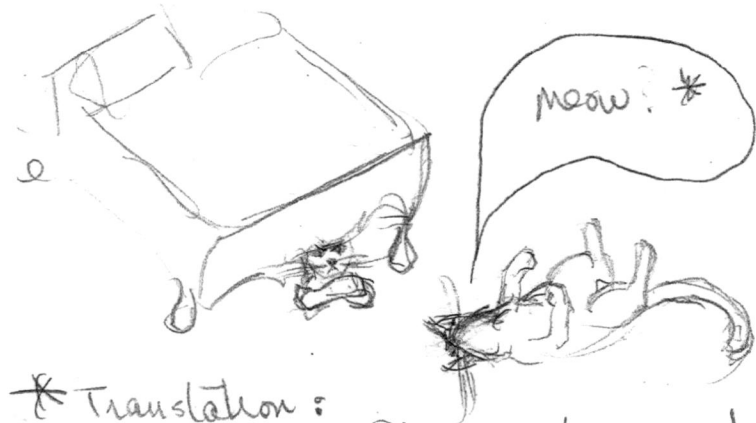

Meow. *

* Translation: "Play with me!!"

Actually, it was a little more than a LITTLE while!

Meow *

* Translation: "Be gone
small nuisance."

Meow *

* Translation: "Play with me!"

9

Over time, as is often the case, things worked out.

FOOD

WATER

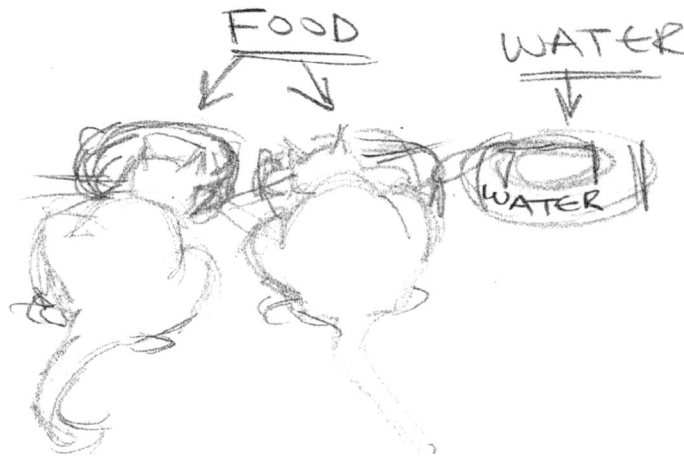

WATER

Now Max and Bernie sleep, eat, and play together. I sleep, eat, and play with them, too.

← PLAY

They have lots of toys.  Here are some favorites:

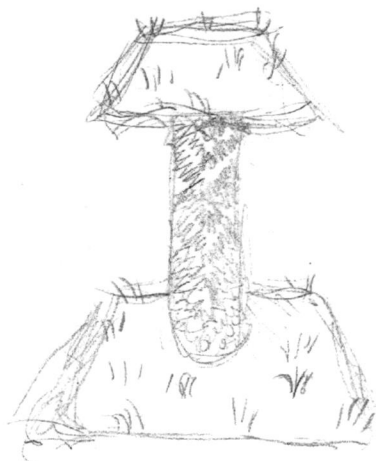

Balls with bells

The fur mouse

The cloth mice
(catnip optional)

The carpeted scratching post.

Some toys were not originally meant to be toys.

The dropped cotton ball. Joy!

The telephone cord.

The empty carton

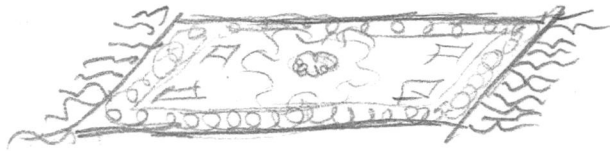

← The fringe on the rug.

The brush

A cat's diet is very important to its health and well-being. I give Bernie and Max half a six-ounce can of wet food each—once in the morning, and once in the evening. I also make a bowl of dry food available to them at all times.

Here are some proper feeding tips:

1. Speak to a veterinarian about which diet is best for your kitty. She will probably base her decision upon your cat's age, weight, and lifestyle. Some foods are good, but some are like our version of "junk food." Investigate.

2. Try to keep to a schedule. Feed your cat(s) at a specific time. You wouldn't want your meals too early or too late.

3. Variety is very important when feeding cats! Try lots of different flavors. Pay attention to which they prefer. Avoid ones they dislike.

Fresh water is really important! Change it at least once a day.

Unclean water ☹

Fresh, clean water!

Dry food: It comes in many shapes and sizes. For example:

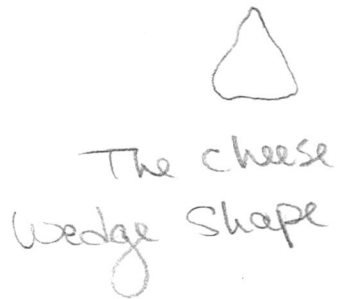

The cheese wedge shape

The pellets

The fishy

Natural Enemy Crackers

Don't forget the treats!

HAPPY HAPPY KITTY

PRETTY PLAYFUL PET TREATS

EAT'EM UPS.

CARTON O' COD

CARTON O' COD

TROUT TREATS

TASTY TUNA TIDBITS

MARLIN MANIA

SQUID SURPRISE

Some treats were not originally meant to be treats:

Anchovies OR Sausage

Thanksgiving dinner

Flowers + Plants

Bugs

Mmm... Mmm Good!

Like people, cats have their own special habits and unique behaviors.

**HIDING PLACES:**

Under the bed is one of Max's favorite places.

MAX

Bernie is not as shy as Max, so he hides less. But if he becomes frightened by my vacuuming or by a visitor to whom he's not accustomed, he usually joins Max under the bed.

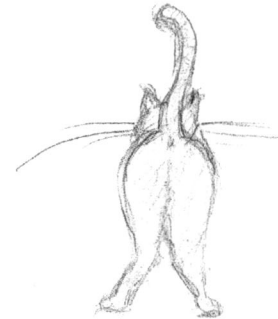

Max also likes the third shelf in the linen closet (often this is also her bedroom).

Another part of caring for a cat is trimming her nails. A special clipper keeps your pet's claws from getting too long and in their way. This is especially important for indoor cats, whose nails don't get as much attention as those of outdoor cats, even with a scratching post.

Bernie doesn't mind having his claws trimmed. Max minds having her hind paws clipped, but she's happy when it's over.

NAIL CLIPPER

PAW

TOE NAIL

★ Important: You can harm your cat if you don't trim her nails properly. Make sure you know what you're doing. If you have any questions, consult a vet or a cat groomer.

## LIKES AND DISLIKES:

Both Bernie and Max like being scratched under their chins and behind their ears.

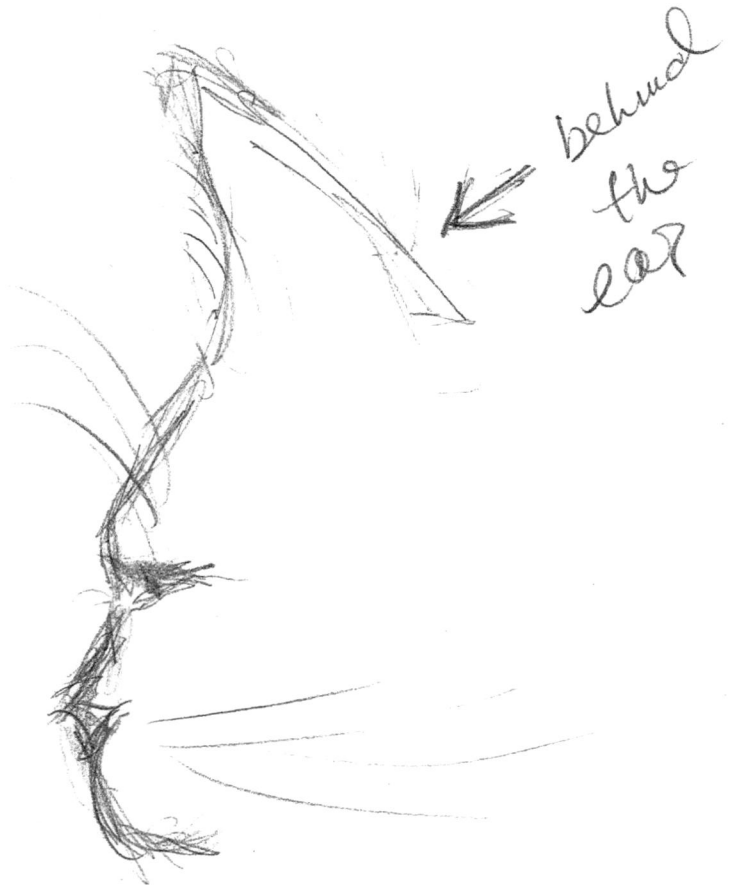

under
the
Chin

behind
the
ear

They also like being brushed with a special grooming brush, which can be bought in any pet shop.

Position they assume when being groomed.

My father, who with my mother adopted three cats, just reminded me about the tummy. It's true! Bernie and Max both love a belly rub.

While Max likes to be stroked, she doesn't like being held. Bernie likes being petted and held.

Max also likes having her tail gently tugged.

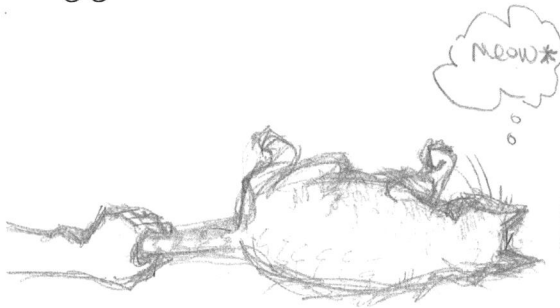

Meow*

\* Translation: "Gee, do I enjoy having my tail gently tugged!"

Bernie especially likes to jump on my lap when I'm sitting in a chair, on the couch, or. . . .

This is Bernie's favorite place to sit on my lap.

Both cats, but especially Max, like to play under the blanket. Sometimes they sleep there, too.

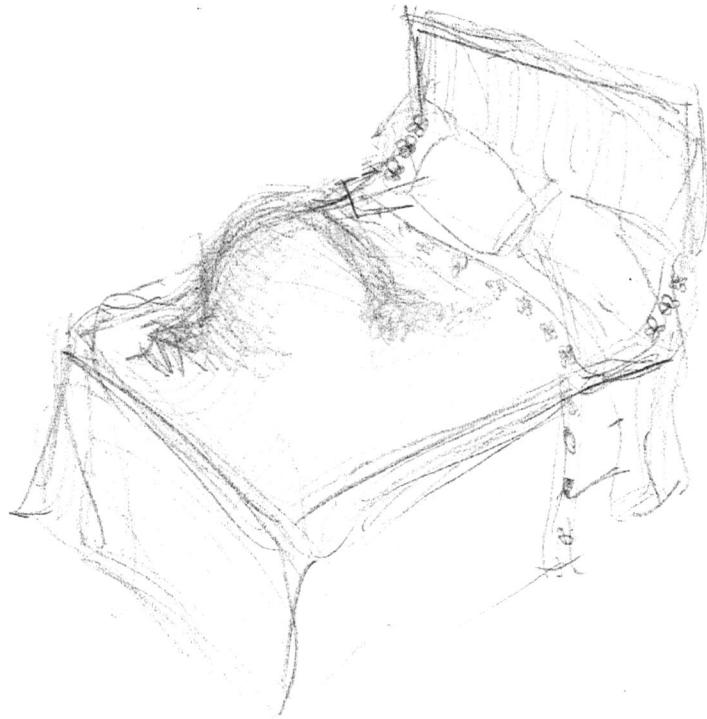

Max auditioning ← for the part of the elephant in The Little Prince

The window sill is a favorite hang-out for both cats.

Max prefers the dry food to the wet.

Max Racing toward the dry food

Bernie prefers the wet food.

Bernie about to savor a bowl of wet food.

Bernie likes to sleep at the head of the bed.

Max likes to sleep at the foot of the bed.

Both Max and Bernie enjoy settling into a pile of freshly washed laundry.

Max and Bernie like to sit in the hall outside the door of my neighbor and her cat, Begonia.

THE END

To cats
and cat lovers
everywhere.

www.ingramcontent.com/pod-product-compliance
Lightning Source LLC
Chambersburg PA
CBHW040453100426

42813CB00022BA/2989